Delight

A WALK THROUGH THE PSALMS

PSALMS 1-30

KRISTIN SCHMUCKER

Delight | A Walk Through the Psalms: Psalms 1-30

The Daily Grace Co. exists to equip disciples to know and love God and His Word by creating beautiful, theologically rich, and accessible resources so that God may be glorified and the gospel made known.

Designed in the United States of America and printed in China.

Unlock Your Digital Study

Did you know you can access your new study right from your phone?
Follow these simple steps, and you will be on your way to diving deeper into God's Word.

Download The Daily Grace Co. App

AVAILABLE FOR FREE IN THE APP STORE AND GOOGLE PLAY

Search for Your New Study

LOCATE YOUR STUDY IN THE DAILY GRACE CO. APP

- Select the "Studies" tab found at the bottom of the home page in the app.
- Select the pink "+" button to bring up all available studies.
- Click on your new study.

Apply Your Access Code

EMAILED TO YOU AFTER PURCHASE

- Copy the access code from your email, and enter it into the "Unlock Study with Access Code" box found on our app.
- You are all set! Now that you have downloaded the app, found your study, and applied your access code, you can begin your study virtually!
- If you did not receive an email with an access code after the purchase of your new study, check your spam folder. If you still cannot find your access code, contact our Customer Care team at info@thedailygraceco.com.

OTHER APP FEATURES

VIDEOS

COMMUNITY

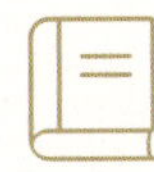
BIBLE

BLOG

PODCAST

AND MORE!

Study Suggestions

We believe that the Bible is true, trustworthy, and timeless and that it is vitally important for all believers. These study suggestions are intended to help you more effectively study Scripture as you seek to know and love God through His Word.

SUGGESTED STUDY TOOLS

- ☐ Bible
- ☐ Double-spaced, printed copy of the Scripture passages that this study covers (You can use a website like www.biblegateway.com to copy the text of a passage and print out a double-spaced copy to be able to mark on easily).
- ☐ Journal to write notes or prayers
- ☐ Pens, colored pencils, and highlighters
- ☐ Dictionary to look up unfamiliar words

HOW TO USE THIS STUDY

Pray

Begin your study time in prayer. Ask God to reveal Himself to you, help you understand what you are reading, and transform you with His Word (Psalm 119:18).

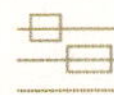

Read Scripture

Before you read what is written in each day of the study itself, read the assigned passages of Scripture for that day. Use your double-spaced copy to circle, underline, highlight, draw arrows, and mark in any way you would like to help you dig deeper as you work through a passage.

Read Study Content

Read the daily written content provided for the current study day.

Respond

Answer the questions that appear at the end of each study day.

How to Study the Bible

The inductive method provides tools for deeper and more intentional Bible study. To study the Bible inductively, work through the steps below after reading background information on the book.

Observation & Comprehension

KEY QUESTION: WHAT DOES THE TEXT SAY?

After reading the daily Scripture in its entirety at least once, begin working with smaller portions of the Scripture. Read a passage of Scripture repetitively, and then mark the following items in the text:

- Key or repeated words and ideas
- Key themes
- Transition words (e.g., therefore, but, because, if/then, likewise, etc.)
- Lists
- Comparisons and contrasts
- Commands
- Unfamiliar words (look these up in a dictionary)
- Questions you have about the text

Interpretation

KEY QUESTION: WHAT DOES THE TEXT MEAN?

Once you have annotated the text, work through the following steps to help you interpret its meaning:

- Read the passage in other versions for a better understanding of the text.
- Read cross-references to help interpret Scripture with Scripture.
- Paraphrase or summarize the passage to check for understanding.
- Identify how the text reflects the metanarrative of Scripture, which is the story of creation, fall, redemption, and restoration.
- Read trustworthy commentaries if you need further insight into the meaning of the passage.

Application

KEY QUESTION: HOW SHOULD THE TRUTH OF THIS PASSAGE CHANGE ME?

Bible study is not merely an intellectual pursuit. The truths about God, ourselves, and the gospel that we discover in Scripture should produce transformation in our hearts and lives. Answer the following questions and prompts as you consider what you have learned in your study:

- What attributes of God's character are revealed in the passage?
- Consider places where the text directly states the character of God, as well as how His character is revealed through His words and actions.
- What do I learn about myself in light of who God is?
- Consider how you fall short of God's character, how the text reveals your sin nature, and what it says about your new identity in Christ.
- How should this truth change me?
- A passage of Scripture may contain direct commands telling us what to do or warnings about sins to avoid in order to help us grow in holiness. Other times, our application flows out of seeing ourselves in light of God's character. As we pray and reflect on how God is calling us to change in light of His Word, we should be asking questions like, "How should I pray for God to change my heart?" and "What practical steps can I take toward cultivating habits of holiness?"

The Attributes of God

Eternal

God has no beginning and no end. He always was, always is, and always will be.

HAB. 1:12 / REV. 1:8 / IS. 41:4

Faithful

God is incapable of anything but fidelity. He is loyally devoted to His plan and purpose.

2 TIM. 2:13 / DEUT. 7:9 / HEB. 10:23

Good

God is pure; there is no defilement in Him. He is unable to sin, and all He does is good.

GEN. 1:31 / PS. 34:8 / PS. 107:1

Gracious

God is kind, giving us gifts and benefits we do not deserve.

2 KINGS 13:23 / PS. 145:8 IS. 30:18

Holy

God is undefiled and unable to be in the presence of defilement. He is sacred and set-apart.

REV. 4:8 / LEV. 19:2 / HAB. 1:13

Incomprehensible and Transcendent

God is high above and beyond human understanding. He is unable to be fully known.

PS. 145:3 / IS. 55:8–9 ROM. 11:33–36

Immutable

God does not change. He is the same yesterday, today, and tomorrow.

1 SAM. 15:29 / ROM. 11:29 JAMES 1:17

Infinite

God is limitless. He exhibits all of His attributes perfectly and boundlessly.

ROM. 11:33–36 / IS. 40:28 PS. 147:5

Jealous

God is desirous of receiving the praise and affection He rightly deserves.

EX. 20:5 / DEUT. 4:23–24 JOSH. 24:19

Just

God governs in perfect justice. He acts in accordance with justice. In Him, there is no wrongdoing or dishonesty.

IS. 61:8 / DEUT. 32:4 / PS. 146:7–9

Loving

God is eternally, enduringly, steadfastly loving and affectionate. He does not forsake or betray His covenant love.

JN. 3:16 / EPH. 2:4–5 / 1 JN. 4:16

Merciful

God is compassionate, withholding from us the wrath that we deserve.

TITUS 3:5 / PS. 25:10 LAM. 3:22–23

Omnipotent

God is all-powerful;
His strength is unlimited.

MAT. 19:26 / JOB 42:1-2
JER. 32:27

Omnipresent

God is everywhere;
His presence is near
and permeating.

PROV. 15:3 / PS. 139:7-10
JER. 23:23-24

Omniscient

God is all-knowing;
there is nothing
unknown to Him.

PS. 147:4 / I JN. 3:20
HEB. 4:13

Patient

God is long-suffering and enduring. He gives ample opportunity for people to turn toward Him.

ROM. 2:4 / 2 PET. 3:9 / PS. 86:15

Self-Existent

God was not created but exists by His power alone.

PS. 90:1-2 / JN. 1:4 / JN. 5:26

Self-Sufficient

God has no needs and depends on nothing, but everything depends on God.

IS. 40:28-31 / ACTS 17:24-25
PHIL. 4:19

Sovereign

God governs over all things; He is in complete control.

COL. 1:17 / PS. 24:1-2
1 CHRON. 29:11-12

Truthful

God is our measurement of what is fact. By Him we are able to discern true and false.

JN. 3:33 / ROM. 1:25 / JN. 14:6

Wise

God is infinitely knowledgeable and is judicious with His knowledge.

IS. 46:9-10 / IS. 55:9 / PROV. 3:19

Wrathful

God stands in opposition to all that is evil. He enacts judgment according to His holiness, righteousness, and justice.

PS. 69:24 / JN. 3:36 / ROM. 1:18

Timeline of Scripture

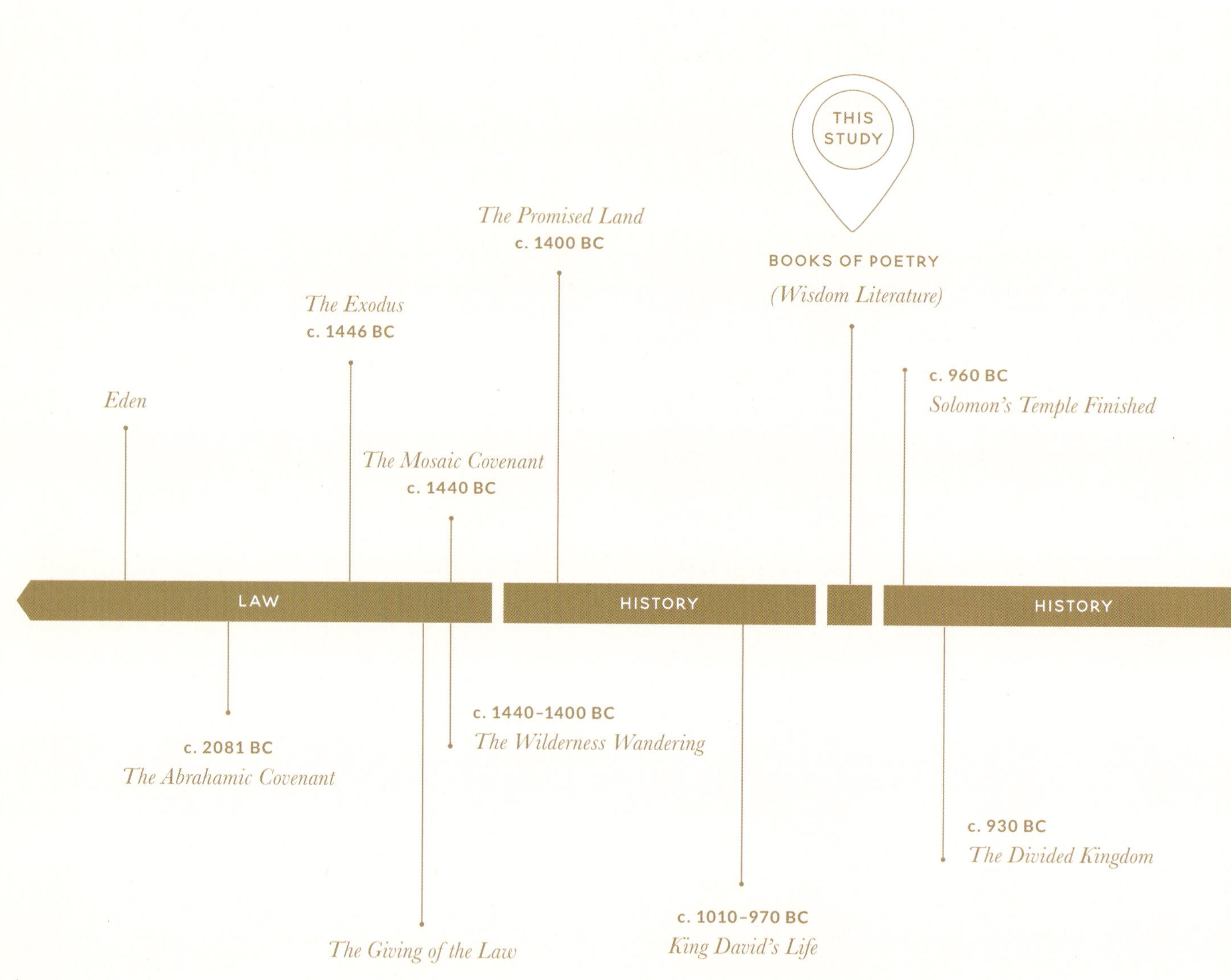

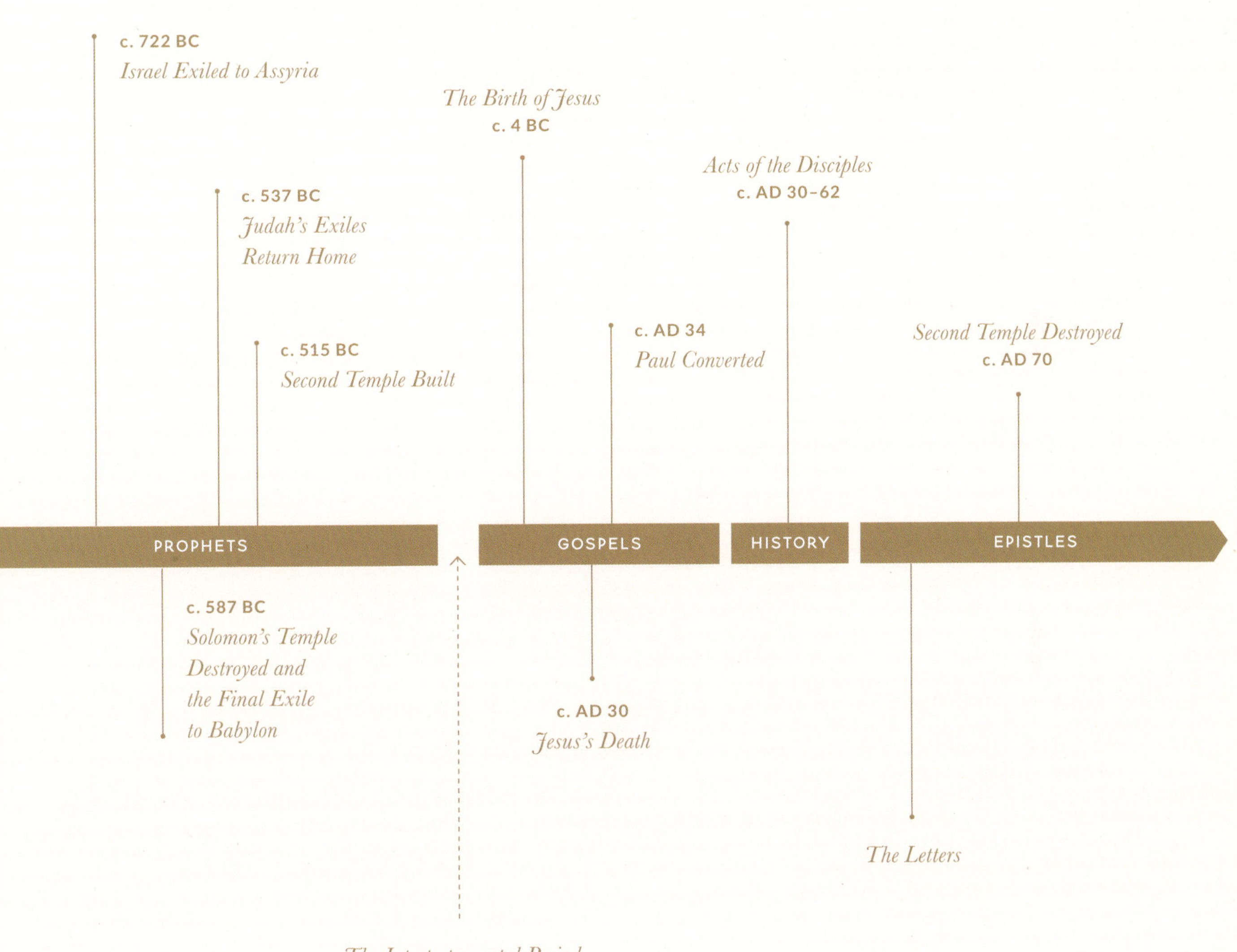
c. 722 BC
Israel Exiled to Assyria
c. 537 BC
Judah's Exiles Return Home
c. 515 BC
Second Temple Built
The Birth of Jesus
c. 4 BC
Acts of the Disciples
c. AD 30–62
c. AD 34
Paul Converted
Second Temple Destroyed
c. AD 70
PROPHETS
GOSPELS
HISTORY
EPISTLES
c. 587 BC
Solomon's Temple Destroyed and the Final Exile to Babylon
c. AD 30
Jesus's Death
The Letters
The Intertestamental Period

Metanarrative of Scripture

Creation

In the beginning, God created the universe. He made the world and everything in it. He created humans in His own image to be His representatives on the earth.

Fall

The first humans, Adam and Eve, disobeyed God by eating from the fruit of the Tree of Knowledge of Good and Evil. Their disobedience impacted the whole world. The punishment for sin is death, and because of Adam's original sin, all humans are sinful and condemned to death.

Redemption

God sent His Son to become a human and redeem His people. Jesus Christ lived a sinless life but died on the cross to pay the penalty for sin. He resurrected from the dead and ascended into heaven. All who put their faith in Jesus are saved from death and freely receive the gift of eternal life.

Restoration

One day, Jesus Christ will return again and restore all that sin destroyed. He will usher in a new heaven and new earth where all who trust in Him will live eternally with glorified bodies in the presence of God.

Table of Contents

READ PSALM 1

The Psalms open with a psalm of wisdom and a contrast of the righteous and the wicked. Some have even suggested that the start of this psalm is as much a description of Jesus as it is an admonition for us to live like Him. The psalm opens like the Sermon on the Mount (Matthew 5) with the word "blessed," and the psalmist will describe the blessed, or righteous, person for us. We first see what the blessed man does not do. He does not dwell with sinners or become accustomed to sin. The words "walk," "stand," and "sit" show us a progression of how we can become comfortable with our sin and the sin of this world. At first, one simply walks by sin and takes a glance, then one stands near wickedness, and soon one will find themselves sitting down and fully comfortable with unrighteousness. Sin is a slippery slope, so we must stay far from it.

The blessed one delights in God's Word and finds their strength in God alone. They also meditate on it. The Hebrew here gives the sense of constantly meditating. God's Word should be always on our minds so that it can penetrate our hearts. The righteous are like trees planted by the living water. These are not wild trees that grow wherever the wind lays seed, but these are chosen trees, intentionally planted and cultivated, just as we are by our loving Father. These verses call us to abide (John 15) as we see that this tree brings forth fruit in season, and its leaf does not wither. This tree is fruit-bearing and evergreen. The seasons of life come, and each season brings new fruit. Even the darkest seasons produce fruit in the life of the believer.

The righteous person prospers in all that he does. We may not think that in what we have done we have prospered, but even our failures are prosperity in God's economy because He is working them for our good (Romans 8:28).

Just as Jesus reminded us in Matthew 5, God views things differently than this world. This success is measured by God's standards and not our own. The wicked pictured here are the opposite of the righteous, but this is our mission field—those who do not know the hope that we have found and that has found us.

May we be like Jesus. May we be like the righteous One who delights in God's Word, meditates on it all day long, abides in the Lord, bears fruit, and prospers in all—not because of anything that we have done but because of the power of our God in us.

MAY WE BE LIKE THE RIGHTEOUS ONE

who delights in God's Word.

WHAT DOES IT MEAN TO DELIGHT IN THE LAW OF THE LORD?
IN WHAT WAYS DO YOU DELIGHT IN THE LORD'S INSTRUCTION TO YOU?

THINK ABOUT WHAT IT MEANS TO BE "PLANTED BESIDE FLOWING STREAMS."
DO YOU FIND YOURSELF "PLANTED" NEAR THE LIFE-GIVING WATERS OF GOD'S WORD?

IN WHAT WAYS DOES THIS PSALM ENCOURAGE
YOU TO LIVE A RIGHTEOUS AND HOLY LIFE?

WEEK ONE / DAY TWO

Refuge

Refuge

READ PSALM 2

Psalm 1 began with a contrast of the righteous and the wicked, and Psalm 2 shows us the righteous One and the wickedness of the world but also the blessing for those who trust in Jesus. This psalm is the first Messianic Psalm, and it is quoted or referenced in the New Testament at least eighteen times. No other psalm is quoted this much, so we can be sure that the message is an important one.

This psalm shows the world system opposing our God and the Anointed One (Jesus, the Messiah). This concept is not a new one. From the beginning of the world, man in his pride has been guilty of opposing the Lord. However, we are reminded that though the world comes against our God, the battle is already won, and Jesus is the victor. Though man rebels, God will reign victorious. From the beginning, man has rebelled, and yet God has extended mercy for those who would turn to Him.

Here the psalmist gives a beatitude for those who will trust and find refuge in the Lord. Those who reject the Lord will face judgment, but there is grace and mercy for those who place their faith in the King of kings. Our sovereign God is just and holy and also merciful and loving. We stand in awe of who He is and the grace that has been lavished on us as His people.

OUR SOVEREIGN GOD *is just and holy* AND ALSO MERCIFUL *and loving.*

HOW DOES VERSE 1 GIVE YOU INSIGHT INTO THE RESULTS OF THE FALL AND SIN ENTERING INTO THE WORLD?

DOES THIS PSALM GROW YOUR CONFIDENCE IN THE LORD, THAT HE IS SOVEREIGN AND WILL ALWAYS ENACT JUSTICE?

MEDITATE ON THE LINE: "ALL WHO TAKE REFUGE IN HIM ARE HAPPY." SPEND SOME TIME IN PRAYER, ASKING THAT GOD WOULD CONTINUALLY TEACH YOU TO TAKE REFUGE IN HIM.

Helps for the Helpless

READ PSALM 3

Our God is help for the helpless. Psalm 3 is a psalm of David written when David was fleeing from his son Absalom as Absalom sought to take over the kingdom and kill David. David came boldly to the Lord and poured out the burdens of his heart. David was facing many foes, and by the world's standard, there was no hope for him. People looked at him and thought that not even God could help David (verse 2). But these people must not have known our God. Our God is the help of the helpless, and the impossible is possible with Him (Matthew 19:26, Jeremiah 32:17). David chose to place his trust in the Lord who had made an everlasting covenant with him (2 Samuel 7). He knew that the Lord would keep His promises.

David proclaimed the truth of who God is, and he trusted God for victory. David proclaimed that God was a shield around him. In the original Hebrew during the time period that this was written, the word for "shield" was much deeper than what we know of the word today. It conveys a surrounding on all sides. It was not just a shield in front but a piece of armor that surrounded every side of a soldier. It reminds us that we are being protected from every side—protected from the enemy on the outside and all the problems of life. We are even protected from the inside and from our own minds and hearts within us that do not always align with the truth. He is our shield on every side.

The same God who was with David is with us as well. We can be assured of victory because of who He is. We know that He will keep His promises, and we can rest in His protection. We can live in the victory that only He can give.

OUR GOD IS THE *help of the helpless,* AND THE IMPOSSIBLE IS *possible with Him.*

HOW DOES UNDERSTANDING DAVID'S CIRCUMSTANCE WITH ABSALOM HELP YOU BETTER UNDERSTAND THE MEANING OF THIS PSALM?

IN WHAT WAYS DOES THIS PSALM BOLSTER YOUR CONFIDENCE THAT GOD WILL PREVAIL IN DIFFICULT CIRCUMSTANCES?

DWELL ON VERSE 5. IN WHAT WAYS HAVE YOU EXPERIENCED THE LORD SUSTAINING YOU?

WEEK ONE / DAY FOUR

Answer Me When I Call

Answer Me When I Call

READ PSALM 4

Psalm 4 is often called the evening psalm to complement the morning psalm of Psalm 3. The psalm begins with David coming to the Lord and pleading with God to not only hear but to answer. David pleads on the basis of who God is and all that He has done. We can learn much about prayer by observing the psalms. In many translations, David uses the title, "O God of my righteousness," which is only used in this psalm and gives God the glory for any good that is in David. David remembers God's past faithfulness to him, which gives him confidence to trust the Lord. Charles Spurgeon said, "He will never cease to help us until we cease to need." We can be confident that the Lord has chosen us, that He will see us through, and that He will hear us when we call to Him. Whatever we face, we can stand in confidence before men because we have first faced our God. Other people may come against us, but we must be sure to keep our hearts pure before the Lord.

The favor of God and the joy that He gives is better than anything that this world has to offer. Nothing in this world satisfies like Jesus. In 1632, Alexander Grosse wrote, "Where Christ reveals himself there is satisfaction in the slenderest portion, and without Christ there is emptiness in the greatest fullness." The words are just as true today as they were generations ago when they were written. Jesus is the only One who satisfies. He is the only One who brings joy and the only One who gives rest and peace. With Jesus, we can say, "It is well with my soul."

NOTHING IN THIS WORLD *satisfies like Jesus.*

MEDITATE ON VERSE 3. WHAT DOES IT MEAN THAT GOD HAS "SET APART THE FAITHFUL FOR HIMSELF," AND WHAT DOES THAT LOOK LIKE?

REREAD VERSE 4. IN WHAT WAYS CAN YOU BE ANGRY AND NOT SIN?

HOW DOES VERSE 8 GROW YOUR UNDERSTANDING OF GOD? DO YOU TRUST IN THE SECURITY HE PROVIDES?

I Will Wait

READ PSALM 5

In the fifth psalm, we see an urgent and expectant prayer from David. We are not given any insight into the exact situation during which the psalm was written, but it is clearly a difficult time for David. Perhaps, as in Psalms 3 and 4, he is fleeing from Absalom, or perhaps it is something different. Whatever the case may be, we see David here with a troubled heart.

David comes to the Lord with urgency and asks the Lord to hear him and answer his requests. When he asks God to consider, he is asking God to hear his prayer and then do what is best. We should come to the Lord in the same way. We should pour out our hearts and our requests before the Lord and then ask Him to do what is best. We must recognize, like David, that we do not always know what is best for ourselves, but the Lord always knows what is best for us.

David also came expectantly. He believed the Lord would answer. In verse 3, David pleads his case before the Lord, and then he watches and waits expectantly for an answer. David calls for God's justice and holiness to prevail against sin and points out that we come to God based on His mercy and not our own merit. We can come to God because of Jesus (Hebrews 10:19–20). Like David, we must recognize that it is His mercy that has delivered us, and then we plead for His way and not our own way. We want His will to be done and not our own will—His kingdom, not our kingdoms. And after we have prayed to Him, we can rejoice because the Lord blesses the righteous with favor like a shield that surrounds on all sides. No matter what enemy we have, we know that our God will go with us.

WE SHOULD POUR OUT *our hearts and our requests* BEFORE THE LORD AND THEN *ask Him to do what is best.*

WHAT CAN YOU LEARN ABOUT PRAYING EXPECTANTLY FROM THIS PSALM?

IN VERSE 8, DAVID ASKS GOD TO LEAD HIM IN HIS RIGHTEOUSNESS. WHY MIGHT THAT ATTITUDE BE IMPORTANT? SPEND SOME TIME IN PRAYER, ASKING THAT GOD WOULD LEAD YOU IN HIS RIGHTEOUSNESS.

MEDITATE ON VERSE 11. WHAT ARE SOME REASONS THAT THE LORD'S REFUGE IS WORTHY OF REJOICING? SPEND SOME TIME IN PRAYER, PRAISING GOD FOR HIS GOODNESS AND FOR PROVIDING YOU WITH REFUGE.

WHAT WAS YOUR FAVORITE PASSAGE FROM THE WEEK?

Take some time to dwell on the Word by writing out the passage in the space provided.

Scripture Memory

FOR YOU ARE NOT A
GOD WHO DELIGHTS
IN WICKEDNESS;
EVIL CANNOT
DWELL WITH YOU.

Psalm 5:4

Week One Reflection

SUMMARIZE THE MAIN POINTS FROM THIS WEEK'S SCRIPTURE READINGS.

WHAT DID YOU OBSERVE FROM THIS WEEK'S PASSAGES ABOUT GOD AND HIS CHARACTER?

WHAT DO THIS WEEK'S PASSAGES REVEAL ABOUT THE CONDITION OF MANKIND AND YOURSELF?

Read Psalms 1-5

HOW DO THESE PASSAGES POINT TO THE GOSPEL?

HOW SHOULD YOU RESPOND TO THESE PASSAGES? WHAT SPECIFIC ACTION STEPS CAN YOU TAKE THIS WEEK TO APPLY THEM IN YOUR LIFE?

WRITE A PRAYER IN RESPONSE TO YOUR STUDY OF GOD'S WORD. ADORE GOD FOR WHO HE IS, CONFESS SINS HE REVEALED IN YOUR OWN LIFE, ASK HIM TO EMPOWER YOU TO WALK IN OBEDIENCE, AND PRAY FOR ANYONE WHO COMES TO MIND AS YOU STUDY.

The Lord Has Heard My Plea

READ PSALM 6

Psalm 6 is considered to be the first of the Penitential Psalms. We are not sure exactly at what point in David's life it was written, but it is clear that he was very distressed. David pleads with God not to discipline him in anger, but Hebrews 12:5-11 reminds us that God only ever disciplines out of love. His correction, as a loving Father, is always meant to grow and mature us. David pleads his own weakness and God's infinite strength, which is a good plea for us as well. At the end of verse 3, David cries, "Lord—how long?"

Certainly, there have been times in our own lives when we have felt the same ache—times when we have felt that ache of uncertainty in our hearts. But our God knows exactly how long our trials will last. He will not allow us to suffer even one day too long. Our God always shows up at just the right time. He delivered Israel from Egypt on the very day He had appointed (Exodus 12:41). He sent Jesus for us at the right time (Romans 5:6–8). He delivered David at the right moment. And He will do the same for us. David's emotions were telling him many things, but the truth of God's Word never changed. Through much of this psalm, David is distressed. But by the last three verses, something has changed, and David knows that he has not been forgotten and God has heard his prayers.

We serve the same great God that David did. He is working behind the scenes in ways that we do not know and could never comprehend. He will be faithful. He will hear our cries. And at just the right time, He will deliver us.

OUR GOD KNOWS EXACTLY *how long our trials will last.* HE WILL NOT ALLOW US TO SUFFER *even one day too long.*

WHAT DOES THIS PSALM TEACH YOU ABOUT THE CHARACTER AND NATURE OF GOD?

MEDITATE ON VERSE 9. IN WHAT WAYS DOES THIS VERSE ENCOURAGE YOU TO RUN TO THE LORD IN PRAYER? DOES THIS VERSE CHANGE YOUR ATTITUDE OR PERCEPTION OF PRAYER?

SPEND SOME TIME IN PRAYER, ASKING THAT GOD WOULD GROW YOUR CONFIDENCE THAT HE HEARS YOUR PRAYERS AND THAT HIS STEADFAST LOVE WOULD CONTINUE TO DELIVER YOU FROM SUFFERING.

WEEK TWO / DAY TWO

Deliver Me

Deliver Me

READ PSALM 7

Charles Spurgeon has called this psalm "The Psalm of the Slandered Saint." This psalm of David is his response to false accusations made against him. The song was sung because of the words of Cush, who was a man who flattered Saul and slandered David. When we find ourselves in a situation where falsehoods are being told about us, we can find comfort in these words. We must remember that when we are wrongly accused, God is our refuge. No matter what life brings, we can run to Him for help and strength. He will never fail us.

In verses 3–5, David pleads his innocence while also checking his heart and showing his humility before the Lord. Beginning in verse 6, we see David plead with the Lord to "rise up" and take action against the enemies. Our God will work on our behalf. Luke 18:7 tells us that He will give justice to the elect. David did not take the situation into His own hands, but he placed it into the Lord's hands. David's words are a reminder for us to do the same. We can trust the Lord to work for us. The indictment of the wicked is great, and judgment is promised for those who reject the Lord. Sin always catches up to a person. We will reap what we sow (Galatians 6:7).

The end of the psalm concludes with praise to the One who delivers the believer from every attack of the enemy. We can praise the Lord because we know that He will be faithful to us. He is our deliverer.

OUR GOD KNOWS EXACTLY
how long our trials will last.
HE WILL NOT ALLOW US TO SUFFER
even one day too long.

THINK ABOUT THE WAY DAVID SEARCHES HIMSELF IN VERSES 3 – 5. WHAT DOES THIS TEACH YOU ABOUT HUMILITY? ARE YOU WILLING AND ABLE TO SEARCH YOURSELF FOR SINFULNESS?

FOCUS ON VERSE 8 – 11. WHAT DO THESE VERSES SAY ABOUT GOD AS A JUDGE? DO YOU TRUST IN THE LORD'S RIGHTEOUS JUDGMENT? DO YOU BELIEVE THAT HE IS PERFECTLY JUST?

IN VERSE 17, DAVID COMMITS TO PRAISING THE LORD BECAUSE HE IS WORTHY TO BE PRAISED. HOW DOES THIS ENCOURAGE YOU TO PRAISE GOD BECAUSE HE IS GOOD DURING TIMES OF PERSECUTION AND SUFFERING?

Our God

READ PSALM 8

He is higher. He is majestic. And His ways are greater than we could even imagine—yet He loves us. The beauty of Psalm 8 is the beauty of the gospel. The perfect God of heaven came down to earth and died for sinful men that we might partake in His righteousness (2 Corinthians 5:21). The psalm begins and ends the same way—with the psalmist overwhelmed and in awe of the majesty and glory of God. And yet, from the start, we see the sweet truth that this sovereign God of Creation is our God. He is high above us, and yet He is personal.

Though He is great, even little children can praise Him and see the enemy defeated. From Moses in a basket to young Samuel to David and Goliath, Scripture is full of accounts of young people. But it would be a young baby in a manger who would come and defeat the enemy and bring salvation. We are like grains of sand compared to the universe, and yet He has loved us. He has chosen us in Him before the foundation of the world (Ephesians 1:4). As we look at or consider the heavens and all that is created, we cannot help but be overwhelmed that He chose us.

"The work of your fingers," gives the connotation of a skilled embroiderer or the artisan of a tapestry. We are the work of His fingers as well. Like the intricate weaving of a fine tapestry, carefully and skillfully crafted together, we are the work of His hands. We see only the back of the tapestry, with messy strings and pieces that do not make sense. But He sees the front and the beauty of the finished tapestry. He is higher (Isaiah 55:8–9), and yet He looks on us. We may not always understand what He is doing, but we can trust His skilled hand.

AS WE CONSIDER THE HEAVENS *and all that is created,* WE CANNOT HELP BUT BE *overwhelmed that He chose us.*

MEDITATE ON VERSE 2. WHAT DOES IT SAY ABOUT GOD'S STRENGTH AND CHARACTER THAT HE USES THE MOUTHS OF INFANTS TO ACCOMPLISH HIS PLANS?

OBSERVE THE WORK OF THE LORD'S FINGERS BOTH IN NATURE AND IN YOURSELF. HOW DO THE DETAILS AND INTRICACIES OF WHAT YOU IDENTIFY TEACH YOU ABOUT THE CHARACTER OF GOD?

AFTER READING THIS PSALM, DO YOU FIND THAT YOUR ABILITY TO PRAISE GOD HAS GROWN? SPEND SOME TIME IN PRAYER, PRAISING GOD FOR HIS MAJESTY AND GOODNESS.

WEEK TWO / DAY FOUR

We Will Praise

We Will Praise

READ PSALM 9

With everything I am, I will praise His name. And He will be faithful. Psalm 9 is a psalm of praise to a God who never fails His people. This psalm of David gives us confidence in the character of our God and begins with the psalmist thanking God and praising His name with his whole heart. Verse 1 reminds us of how we should think on all that God has done and remember His deliverance. We should remember all of His wonderful deeds, and truly all of His deeds are wonderful, even the ones that we do not understand.

As we reflect on His faithfulness to us, our praise will continue because He has sovereignly done all things for our good. Verse 2 reminds us that the people of God should be happy people known for their joy no matter what may come. God has defeated David's enemies, and He will be with us as well. Verses 7–8 look forward to the future victory, and we can have confidence in the future because of God's unwavering faithfulness to us in the past. Verses 9–10 are the heart of this psalm. The reminder that our God will not forsake us gives us faith to face whatever lies ahead.

As the people of God, we will never be forsaken. In this world, we may feel forgotten or lonely, but the One who has given His own life for us will never forsake us. We cannot help but praise Him and share with those around us all that He has done for us. We share the message that though He is the just One, He is also the justifier. We share that though we are weak, He is strong, and we are never forgotten. And then we praise Him for who He is and let the joy of our salvation shine out as a light in a dark world.

TRULY ALL OF HIS DEEDS

are wonderful,

EVEN THE ONES THAT WE

do not understand.

THE FIRST TWO VERSES OF THIS PSALM DENOTE AN ACTIVE CHOICE THAT DAVID COMMITS TO MAKE—HE WILL GIVE THANKS. ARE YOU ABLE TO PRAISE GOD AMID DIFFICULTY? SPEND SOME TIME IN PRAYER, ASKING THAT GOD WOULD GROW YOUR THANKFULNESS AND FAITH IN HIM.

MEDITATE ON VERSES 9 AND 10. WHAT DOES IT MEAN THAT THE LORD IS A STRONGHOLD? DO YOU TRUST THAT THE LORD WILL ALWAYS PROTECT YOU?

REREAD VERSE 14. WHAT DOES IT MEAN TO REJOICE IN GOD'S SALVATION? HOW DOES REJOICING IN GOD'S SALVATION GIVE US A PROPER UNDERSTANDING OF THE TRIALS WE SUFFER ON EARTH?

He Sees

READ PSALM 10

Our God will never forsake His own, and we can praise Him right in the midst of this life. This psalm does not indicate its author, though it is commonly believed to be a psalm of David and a continuation of Psalm 9. The psalm opens with a plea of why the Lord has hidden Himself. The beauty of David is not that he was without struggle but that he ran to God again and again. He allowed his struggles and even his own sin to only draw him closer to the Father. The Lord never leaves His people, and in the moments when He seems distant, we can take comfort that He will walk through the fire with us, hidden but still present. There may be times when it seems to us that He has hidden Himself, and we do not understand His plan. And yet, even then, we can know that He is still there.

This psalm describes the wicked. The description shows their many sins, but all are rooted in pride. Our sin is also rooted in pride and a deeper love for ourselves than for God. Pride keeps us from seeking the Lord (verse 4), and the wicked are characterized by living as if there is no god but themselves. *Lord, let it not be true of us.*

In verse 12, the psalmist cries out to God in prayer. Two different Hebrew names of God are used here. "LORD" here is Jehovah or Yahweh, the covenant name of God. "God" here is translated from the Hebrew word for God, "El." The Psalmist is praying for God to rescue him in His strength, power, and might as he cries out, "O LORD, keep your covenant and promises to me. O God Almighty, rescue me in your mighty strength. The psalmist comes boldly in faith, and we can as well (Hebrews 4:16). We are pleading on the basis of who He is, and as we cry out to Him, our hearts are reminded that He is faithful, and He will be faithful to us as well. The psalm ends with a song of thanksgiving for all He has done, all He will do, and for who He is. This faithful, covenant-keeping, almighty God hears the cries of His people.

We come in prayer not to plead our case but to plead His character. We cry out to Him, "Lord, You are faithful; be faithful to me. Lord, You are the Comforter; comfort me." He has been faithful in the past, and we can be sure that He will be faithful again.

WE CAN KNOW THAT

He is still there.

REFLECT ON SOME INSTANCE IN YOUR LIFE WHEN GOD MAY HAVE FELT FAR AWAY. HOW DOES THIS PSALM BRING CLARITY TO SUCH SITUATIONS? DO YOU TRUST THAT THE LORD WILL NOT FORSAKE YOU?

REREAD VERSE 17. IN WHAT WAYS DOES THIS VERSE GIVE YOU HOPE AND COMFORT IN THE CHARACTER OF GOD?

THINK ABOUT WHAT IT MEANS TO "PLEAD THE CHARACTER" OF GOD IN PRAYERS. AS YOU READ THIS PSALM, SPEND SOME TIME IN PRAYER, PRAISING GOD FOR HIS GOOD CHARACTER AND THE ATTENTION HE GIVES TO THOSE IN DISTRESS. PLEAD HIS CHARACTER.

WHAT WAS YOUR FAVORITE PASSAGE FROM THE WEEK?

Take some time to dwell on the Word by writing out the passage in the space provided.

Scripture Memory

I WILL THANK THE LORD
WITH ALL MY HEART;
I WILL DECLARE ALL YOUR
WONDROUS WORKS.

Psalm 9:1

Week Two Reflection

SUMMARIZE THE MAIN POINTS FROM THIS WEEK'S SCRIPTURE READINGS.

WHAT DID YOU OBSERVE FROM THIS WEEK'S PASSAGES ABOUT GOD AND HIS CHARACTER?

WHAT DO THIS WEEK'S PASSAGES REVEAL ABOUT THE CONDITION OF MANKIND AND YOURSELF?

Read Psalms 6-10

HOW DO THESE PASSAGES POINT TO THE GOSPEL?

HOW SHOULD YOU RESPOND TO THESE PASSAGES? WHAT SPECIFIC ACTION STEPS CAN YOU TAKE THIS WEEK TO APPLY THEM IN YOUR LIFE?

WRITE A PRAYER IN RESPONSE TO YOUR STUDY OF GOD'S WORD. ADORE GOD FOR WHO HE IS, CONFESS SINS HE REVEALED IN YOUR OWN LIFE, ASK HIM TO EMPOWER YOU TO WALK IN OBEDIENCE, AND PRAY FOR ANYONE WHO COMES TO MIND AS YOU STUDY.

We Will Trust

READ PSALM 11

Faith > Logic. In this psalm, David is in a bad situation. He is likely fleeing from Saul, who was seeking to take his life. It was a serious time, and this psalm is a psalm of confidence in the Lord. Our situations so often sway our emotions and even our trust in the Lord, but David reminds us in this psalm that even when the situation seems hopeless and logic would tell us to throw in the towel, even then we must trust the Lord. This psalm reminds us that we walk by faith and not by sight (2 Corinthians 5:7).

When we look at our own situations, it seems hopeless. But our God sees what we cannot see. Every part of our lives is a part of His sovereign and perfect plan. We see our lives as a series of good and bad things, but His perspective is not our perspective. He sees what we do not see. And He can take the worst things to bring about the best things (Romans 8:28). So we trust Him. We trust that He will make our paths straight (Proverbs 3:5–6). We say, "Come what may, we will trust You." And we know that come what may, He will be faithful. Some will tell us to flee (verse 1), and some will ask what the righteous can do (verse 3). And we respond that we will trust Him.

We can boldly say, "If God is for us, who can be against us?" (Romans 8:31). We can be confident that He will use trials to refine us and bring justice because He is just. And we look forward to the day when we will see His face and dwell in His presence (Psalm 140:13). The trials will be over, and we will see and know with everything we are that we did not trust Him in vain.

EVERY PART OF OUR LIVES
is a part of His sovereign
AND PERFECT PLAN

SPEND SOME TIME THINKING ABOUT YOUR ALLEGIANCE TO FAITH AND LOGIC. TO WHICH DO YOU HOLD FAST? DOES YOUR FAITH IN GOD TRIUMPH OVER EARTHLY LOGIC?

WHAT DOES THIS PSALM TEACH YOU ABOUT WHAT THE LORD DESPISES? HOW DOES THIS EXPAND YOUR UNDERSTANDING OF WHO GOD IS?

WHAT DOES THIS PSALM TEACH YOU ABOUT WHAT THE LORD LOVES? DOES THIS PSALM ENCOURAGE YOU TO FLEE FROM SIN AND UNRIGHTEOUSNESS?

WEEK THREE / DAY TWO

His Word Will Never Fail

His Word Will Never Fail

READ PSALM 12

We are weak, but He is strong. We are faithless, but He is faithful. In this psalm, David laments that the faithful remnant is dwindling. The scene he described does not sound much different than our own day with people lying, flattering, and celebrating sin. This psalm contrasts man's words with God's Word. Humans speak lies and lift themselves up, covering their sin. They speak flattery that manipulates people and situations.

God's faithful people may find themselves in suffering, but verse 5 reminds us that God hears the oppression of the needy. God hears the affliction of His people like a prayer without words. He sees what we are facing, even when we feel as though we have no strength to even pray. And at just the right moment, He will come. He will arise and come to our rescue, and He will give us rest and safety. Our God will arise for us. He will make us secure and fulfill our longings. Man's words will fail, but God's Word will never fail us. His words are pure. His words have been tried and tested and have proven true time and time again. His words will never fail. Man's words are weak; His Word is strong. Man's words lie; His Word is truth. Man's words wound; His Word heals.

When the words of this world fail us, we can run to His Word that will never fail. Life in this world is difficult, but we can take heart because He has already overcome the world (John 16:33). In a world that is against us, our God is for us.

GOD HEARS THE AFFLICTION *of His people like a* PRAYER WITHOUT WORDS.

REREAD VERSES 3 AND 4. WHAT DO THESE VERSES TELL YOU ABOUT THE POWER OF OUR WORDS?

MEDITATE ON VERSE 6. DO YOU LOVE THE LORD'S WORDS?
DO YOU TRUST THEM TO BE TRUE AND PURE AND BEAUTIFUL?

FOCUS ON THE LAST TWO VERSES OF THIS PSALM. HOW DOES IT COMFORT YOU TO KNOW THAT THE LORD GUARDS HIS PEOPLE DESPITE BEING SURROUNDED BY THE WICKED?

He has Dealt Bountifully with Me

READ PSALM 13

How often have we found ourselves in a situation where our feelings do not line up with the truth? David finds himself in that position in this psalm. The psalm likely was written while David was running from Saul, and the beginning of the psalm shows us what David felt. At the start of the psalm, we see David feeling forgotten. It seems like the Lord is far away and that God has hidden Himself. It is easy for us to feel this way in the midst of our trials. But the Lord made a promise with David, and He would not forsake it (2 Samuel 7). David cried out to the Lord for Him to consider or look on him and answer. David was desperate to be heard by the Lord. David wanted to be rescued for his own sake, as well as for the sake of God's name and glory.

And then, in verse 5, the psalm shifts, and suddenly we move from what David was feeling to what David knew. His fear had been turned to faith. David triumphantly declared that He was trusting in God's steadfast love. He was placing his faith in the covenant-keeping *hesed* love of God, and he was confident that God would keep His Word. He rejoiced in God's salvation and praised God, who had dealt bountifully with him. The Hebrew word here for "bountifully" is *gamal*. It shows that God has been good and dealt bountifully, but it also has the idea of ripening like fruit. You see, David's circumstances had not changed, but God was changing him, growing him, and ripening him. God was dealing bountifully with him.

Our situation does not always change, and God never changes, but He changes us. He grows us and ripens us. He helps us see His goodness and love for us, even when life does not go as planned. So will God forget us? Never! We are His children, and He will never forget us (Isaiah 49:15–16). He will never forget us, but He will grow us so that even in the midst of suffering, we will be able to see His faithfulness and steadfast love for us. May we never allow our feelings to dictate our theology but allow our theology to dictate our feelings. He has dealt bountifully with us.

HE HELPS US SEE HIS *goodness and love for us,* EVEN WHEN LIFE DOES *not go as planned.*

DO YOU SOMETIMES FIND YOURSELF WITH THE SAME FEELINGS OF BEING FORSAKEN THAT DAVID FELT? HOW DOES THE END OF THIS PSALM ENCOURAGE YOU WHEN YOUR FEELINGS DO NOT LINE UP WITH THE TRUTH

IN WHAT WAYS DOES DAVID'S CONFIDENCE IN THE LORD AMID TRIALS GROW YOUR ABILITY AND DESIRE TO PRAISE THE LORD WHILE EXPERIENCING DIFFICULTY?

THINK ABOUT WHAT "BOUNTIFUL" MEANS. HOW DOES THIS PSALM CHALLENGE YOUR VIEWS ABOUT WHAT IS GOOD AND BOUNTIFUL FOR US?

WEEK THREE / DAY FOUR

He Seeks Us

He Seeks Us

READ PSALM 14

This psalm has often been called a psalm on practical atheism. The foolish say in their hearts that there is no God, and men are so prone to live as if there is no God. We think that we know what is best for ourselves, and we often exalt ourselves to the place of God in our own hearts and lives. This psalm shows the condition of every man, and Paul quotes much of it in Romans 3 as he describes the human condition apart from God. In ourselves, we can do nothing good (John 15:5), and even the good things we do are often done with skewed motives.

But the Lord changes everything. In ourselves, we do not seek the Lord, but praise God that He sought us and loved us first (1 John 4:19, Romans 5:8). He loved us while we were unlovable, and He paid for our salvation while we were still the enemies of God. This psalm does not end without the sweet hope of Jesus. We make such a mess of our lives, and yet Jesus is our great hope. He does what we could never do. He loved us while we were still sinners and has exchanged our sin for His righteousness (2 Corinthians 5:21).

This world is full of sin and suffering, but there will come a day when sin and suffering will be no more, and our God will restore and redeem everything. He will free us from the captivity of this world and restore us fully to Himself as He defeats sin and death forever and restores His people. For now, we wait with expectation because we know that He will not make us wait a moment too long. We will praise Him in the waiting.

He loved us while were unlovable,

AND HE PAID FOR OUR SALVATION

while we were still enemies of God.

GO AND READ JOHN 15:5. IN WHAT WAYS DO YOU SEE THE PRECEPTS OF THIS VERSE THROUGHOUT PSALM 14?

THINK ABOUT YOUR LIFE BEFORE YOU ACCEPTED CHRIST. DID YOUR FORMER LIFE RESEMBLE THE CHARACTER TRAITS FOUND IN THIS PSALM?

AS YOU MEDITATE ON THIS CHAPTER, ARE YOU ENCOURAGED TO SEEK AFTER THE LORD MORE FERVENTLY?

Near His Heart

READ PSALM 15

Psalm 15 asks, "Who will dwell with the Lord?" It asks this question and then answers it in the verses that follow. This psalm was likely written after the ark of the covenant was returned to Jerusalem, and David reflected on the joyous occasion. This psalm is the description of the righteous. It is not the way of salvation, but it is the way that the saved should live.

So David asks, "Lord, how do we stay near you? How do we abide with you?" David is seeking the Lord and longing to walk in relationship with Him, and we should desire the same. So who dwells with the Lord? The ones who walk blamelessly and do right. This is not a demand for perfection but a command for us to live with integrity. This verse, and the whole psalm, is a pleading for us to be more like Jesus, who is the only One who perfectly possesses all of these traits. As believers, we are constantly in the process of being sanctified and transformed into the image of the Son. So "blamelessness" is a single word that sums up the entire passage. It is not perfection but integrity before the Lord and before men that God desires from us. It is a tender heart that seeks to serve the Lord and responds to the conviction of the Holy Spirit.

We are to speak truth not just with our lips but also in our hearts. We must not dwell on lies about others, about ourselves, or about God. We should not use our words to wound or do wrong to those around us. We should honor those who love the Lord and not promote evil. We should keep our word and deal honestly with our finances. We should live blameless lives not out of duty but as an overflow of gratitude for the grace we have been given. And the Lord promises that when we are dwelling with Him, we will not be moved. The world around us may shift and change, but we stand firm and unmoved in the grace that we have been given. We will not be shaken.

It is not perfection
BUT INTEGRITY BEFORE THE LORD
and before men that
GOD DESIRES FROM US.

IN WHAT WAYS DOES THIS PSALM SHOW YOU HOW TO LIVE WITH INTEGRITY AND GODLINESS?

WHAT ARE SOME OF THE ATTRIBUTES AND ACTIONS LISTED IN THIS PSALM THAT YOU STRUGGLE WITH? SPEND SOME TIME IN PRAYER, ASKING THAT GOD WOULD TRANSFORM YOU INTO JESUS'S LIKENESS.

REREAD THE LAST LINE IN THE PSALM. WHAT DOES IT MEAN TO REMAIN UNSHAKEN? DO YOU FEEL LIKE YOU ARE EASILY SHAKEN OR UNMOVABLE IN YOUR STEWARDSHIP OF GOD'S GRACE?

WHAT WAS YOUR FAVORITE PASSAGE FROM THE WEEK?

Take some time to dwell on the Word by writing out the passage in the space provided.

Scripture Memory

BUT I HAVE TRUSTED
IN YOUR FAITHFUL LOVE;
MY HEART WILL REJOICE IN
YOUR DELIVERANCE.

Psalm 13:5

Week Three Reflection

SUMMARIZE THE MAIN POINTS FROM THIS WEEK'S SCRIPTURE READINGS.

WHAT DID YOU OBSERVE FROM THIS WEEK'S PASSAGES ABOUT GOD AND HIS CHARACTER?

WHAT DO THIS WEEK'S PASSAGES REVEAL ABOUT THE CONDITION OF MANKIND AND YOURSELF?

Read Psalms 11-15

HOW DO THESE PASSAGES POINT TO THE GOSPEL?

HOW SHOULD YOU RESPOND TO THESE PASSAGES? WHAT SPECIFIC ACTION STEPS CAN YOU TAKE THIS WEEK TO APPLY THEM IN YOUR LIFE?

WRITE A PRAYER IN RESPONSE TO YOUR STUDY OF GOD'S WORD. ADORE GOD FOR WHO HE IS, CONFESS SINS HE REVEALED IN YOUR OWN LIFE, ASK HIM TO EMPOWER YOU TO WALK IN OBEDIENCE, AND PRAY FOR ANYONE WHO COMES TO MIND AS YOU STUDY.

He is My Chosen Portion

READ PSALM 16

This is a psalm of joy. It is not about joy in circumstances but of joy in the Lord. Our joy is not dependent on our circumstances but on who He is. In this psalm, David calls to the Lord, who is the One who is with His children. David remembers, and we must as well, that all we have is from the Lord, and if we do good, it is because of His work in us. As followers of the Lord, we are to love the Lord, love His people, and hate wickedness.

At the center of this psalm, verses 5 and 6 serve as a sweet reminder for us. The wording of these verses refers to the events in the book of Joshua and the boundary lines of the Promised Land. Each tribe of Israel was given an inheritance, but for the priests and Levites, their inheritance was not land but the Lord Himself. David says that the Lord is his chosen portion. David is saying, and we should as well, "Lord, there is nothing that I want more than You." The Lord Himself holds our lot. Our life is in His hands, and it could not be in a more secure place. Often, we are tempted to hold our lives ourselves, but it is so much better for Him to have control. In verse 6, David says that the boundary lines have fallen in pleasant places and that his inheritance is beautiful.

The same is true for us. What the Lord has given us is good, even when we do not understand. His ways are so much better than our ways. David had not been given an easy life, yet still, he said that all he had was good. David knew from experience that suffering with the Lord is better than ease without Him. David turned to the Lord night and day, and he found joy in a personal and constant relationship with the Lord. He knew that the Lord was with him, and that was all he needed. Tucked in verses 9–10, we find a prophecy of resurrection and a reminder that it is our Savior who makes this relationship with the Lord a reality to us as believers today.

The psalm ends with verse 11 and a beautiful declaration of joy. This is a now-and-not-yet promise. Now, as we see Him lead us in this life, we find joy in His presence and pleasure in Him. And someday, we will see this promise fully fulfilled for us. So for now, we will wait for the Lord, who is our chosen portion. We will cling to hope and trust that His plan for us is good. We will say with everything that we are, "Lord, there is nothing we want more than You."

OUR LIFE IS IN HIS HANDS, AND IT *could not be in a more secure place.*

WHAT IS THE DIFFERENCE BETWEEN HAVING JOY IN YOUR CIRCUMSTANCES AND JOY IN THE LORD? WHICH ONE WILL GIVE YOU LASTING SATISFACTION?

SPEND SOME TIME IN SELF-EXAMINATION AFTER READING VERSE 2. DO YOU TRULY UNDERSTAND THAT OUR GOODNESS IS SOLELY FROM THE LORD?

MEDITATE ON VERSE 11. HOW DOES THIS VERSE GROW YOUR UNDERSTANDING OF THE IMPORTANCE OF JOY IN THE LORD?

WEEK FOUR / DAY TWO

I Will Call Upon the Lord

I Will Call Upon the Lord

READ PSALM 17

The psalms record for us some of the most beautiful prayers ever prayed. David constantly turned to the Lord in prayer, and we can pray these same prayers as well. In this psalm that was likely written while David was on the run from Saul, David cries out to the Lord to hear and answer, and he is confident that He will. At the beginning of the psalm, David comes asking God to hear his cause after David had searched his heart. We must constantly search our own hearts and motives and align them with God's Word and God's heart. David Guzik paraphrased David's prayer like this: "Lord, I believe my cause is just and I have searched my own heart for deceit. Yet I wait for your vindication, and I want You to do and promote what is right. If I'm not on Your side, move me so that I am." David did not take matters into his own hands—he asked for the Lord to show up in his circumstances. David also pointed out that it is God's Word that kept him from sin in verse 4. It is Scripture that keeps us from sin as well.

The heart of this psalm is found in verses 6–7. David proclaims that he will call upon the Lord because the Lord will answer him. David had complete faith and confidence that God would answer his prayer. When we have seen God answer our prayers time and time again, we will come with fresh faith and confidence that He will do it again. Spurgeon said, "He who has tried the faithfulness of God in hours of need, has great boldness in laying his case before the throne." Prayer grows our faith as we see Him prove Himself faithful to us over and over again.

David then asks God to show His love. We can come to the Lord boldly and ask Him to show His wonderful love. David asks to be protected as the pupil of God's eye, which connotes being cherished and protected, and then he asks to be hidden in the shadow of God's wings. This is a place of safety and protection, just as a hen guards her chicks. It can also remind us of the tabernacle and the wings of the cherubim over the ark of the covenant. Our God can make even our suffering a holy of holies and a place of communion with Him. His presence is found in the midst of our problems. The psalm ends with a declaration of faith as so many of David's psalms do. David looked to the future, but he also trusted God for the present. This psalm urges us to cry to the Lord in prayer and trust that He will be faithful. Then with David, we can say, "Now and forever, Lord, You are faithful. You are the only One who satisfies."

PRAYER GROWS OUR FAITH AS WE SEE
Him prove Himself faithful to us.

REREAD VERSE 5. WHAT DOES IT MEAN TO HAVE OUR STEPS HOLD FAST TO THE LORD'S PATHS? SPEND SOME TIME IN PRAYER, ASKING THAT GOD WOULD GIVE YOU THE STRENGTH TO MAKE YOUR STEPS HOLD FAST TO HIS PATHS.

HOW ARE VERSES 6–7 AN EXAMPLE OF COMPLETE FAITH AND CONFIDENCE IN THE LORD? IN WHAT WAYS DO THESE VERSES STRENGTHEN YOUR FAITH IN GOD?

MEDITATE ON VERSE 15. WHAT DOES IT MEAN TO BE SATISFIED WITH GOD'S PRESENCE? HOW CAN THAT LEVEL OF SATISFACTION BRING ABOUT COMPLETE JOY?

He Rescued Me Because He Delighted in Me

READ PSALM 18

God had promised David that he would be king, and yet Saul chased him. But God was faithful to His promise and would deliver David. Psalm 18 is David's song of praise to our faithful God. The psalm begins with David's declaration of love for the Lord. The Hebrew word for "love" here, *racham*, is very closely related to the Hebrew word for "womb." This love is like a mother's love for her child, tender and compassionate. It is the way God loves us and the way that we should love Him. This plea from David's heart is raw and personal. We do not come to the Lord as One who is far off and disinterested but as the One who knows us personally, who cares, and will come to our rescue.

In verse 2, David lists so many things that God is, and each is prefaced with the word "my." It is a sweet reminder that God's love and care is personal to His children. He is our rock and our strength and stability when life is uncertain. He is our fortress and our stronghold, the One we can run to. He is our shield and protection. He is our deliverer and rescuer. He is our horn and our strength. He is our God, and we can know He will not forsake us. In verse 3, we are reminded that we can walk confidently into any trial because we know that God will be with us. He has been faithful in the past, and He will be faithful again. The words of this psalm remind us that God hears the cry and prayers of His people and acts on their behalf.

Verse 19 is a reminder that He does not rescue us because He has to but because He loves us and delights in us. When we allow this truth to sink into our hearts, our perspective changes. Because David knew of God's love, he could trust even when he did not understand God's plan. David could confidently proclaim the words of verse 30, that God's ways and timing are perfect, that God's Word is sure and He always keeps His promises, and that He will rescue His people.

Verse 31 asks the question, "For who is God besides the Lord?" It is a reminder that there is none like Him. Nothing satisfies like Jesus. Jonathan Edwards said, "All earthly desires are but streams, but God is the ocean." Even deliverance is not as sweet as the deliverer. He alone is who our hearts long for. David did not take matters into his own hands. He waited on the Lord, and he would find that God's ways are so much better than our own.

So in our waiting, we can trust that His way is perfect. We can be confident of His faithfulness and assured of His steadfast love. We can trust Him and know that He is our greatest desire. There is none like Him.

REFLECT ON VERSE 2. DOES THIS VERSE GROW YOUR UNDERSTANDING OF GOD'S CHARACTER? IN WHAT WAYS DOES THIS VERSE COMFORT YOU?

IN WHAT WAYS DO VERSES 7–15 ILLUSTRATE THE POWER AND MIGHT OF THE LORD? WHY IS IT IMPORTANT TO HAVE A PROPER UNDERSTANDING OF GOD'S POWER?

MEDITATE ON VERSE 46. DOES IT BRING YOU JOY TO REMEMBER THAT THE LORD LIVES? HOW MIGHT IT AFFECT OUR RELATIONSHIP WITH GOD IF WE DO NOT SEE HIM AS LIVING AND ACTIVE?

WEEK FOUR / DAY FOUR

The Law of the Lord is Perfect

The Law of the Lord is Perfect

READ PSALM 19

This beautiful psalm shows how God makes Himself known in creation, in His precious Word, and even in our hearts. Our God in grace reveals Himself to us in so many ways. The heavens show His glory, and His Word shows us who He is. The earth shouts out the truth that there is a God and that He is majestic and glorious, and then Scripture introduces Him and shows how He loves us. In the first verses of the psalm, the name for God is "El," which shows His great and majestic power in creation. But when the psalmist speaks of God's Word, the name for God is Jehovah or Yahweh. This is God's covenant name and shows that He is a personal God.

As the psalm goes on, we see the many different functions of God's Word in our lives. God's Word is perfect, and it restores, revives, and refreshes the soul. There is power in the Word of God. God's Word is like water for the thirsty soul. God's Word is living, and it gives life. Scripture is the testimony of the Lord, and it tells us who He is. Who He is changes us and makes us wise. The precepts of the Lord are right, and when we follow the Lord's plan, we will live lives of joy. We can have joy when we see that God's ways are the best ways, and we can trust Him even when we do not understand. God's Word is true, trustworthy, and timeless. God's Word opens our eyes and illuminates our path. God's Word is pure. It has been tested and tried. It has stood the test of time and proven faithful, and it will surely prove faithful for us as well. God's Word is powerful and pure, it is enlightening and enduring, it is forever, and it is faithful.

There should be nothing that we desire more than God's Word because it is there that we find Him. God's Word is better than all of the possessions one could earn, and it is better than all of the pleasures that this world has to offer. David ends this psalm with recognition of his own weakness and sinfulness and of God's constant faithfulness. God's Word reveals our sin, and then God cleanses us and declares us innocent. We are so easily tempted to sin, but we can be assured that because of God's grace, sin no longer has dominion over us (Romans 6:14). The more we draw near to the Lord, the more we see our own weakness, and the sweeter His grace will be to us.

The psalm ends with a prayer that not only our actions but also our words and the thoughts of our hearts be pure and acceptable before the Lord. "Acceptable" is a term used commonly to refer to the condition of a sacrifice, so here we see our words and thoughts as an offering back to the Lord. We come and give our all to our Rock and our Redeemer who has given all for us. In the heavens above, in His precious Word, and in our hearts, our Redeemer is faithful.

THINK ABOUT VERSES 7–8. IN WHAT WAYS DOES THE LORD'S INSTRUCTION RENEW OUR LIVES? HOW DOES IT MAKE US WISE? WHY DOES IT MATTER IF IT IS TRUSTWORTHY?

MEDITATE ON VERSES 10–11. WHY IS THE WORD OF GOD SO PRECIOUS? DOES THIS PSALM GROW YOUR DESIRE TO KNOW GOD'S WORD?

REREAD VERSE 14. WHAT ARE SOME PRACTICAL WAYS THAT YOU CAN CHALLENGE THE WORDS OF YOUR MOUTH AND MEDIATION OF YOUR HEART TO BE PLEASING AND ACCEPTABLE TO GOD?

Before We Call, He Will Answer

READ PSALM 20

Psalm 20 is a song to be sung before battle. The Christian life is often described as a battle (1 Timothy 6:12, Ephesians 6:12), so these words encourage us as we face this life. This is our battle cry. The psalm begins with the people pleading for the Lord to answer in the day of trouble, and verse 6 tells us that He will answer. "Trouble" here means "adversity, affliction, distress," and even "tightness," which gives the feeling of being stuck. And we all have experienced a day of trouble! The people cry for the name of the Lord to be their protection—and we can as well. The name of the Lord is His Word and His character—it is who He is. We call upon the name and character of God to rescue us as well. The beginning verses are prayers by the people for David before he goes into battle, but many scholars have also viewed this as a prophetic prayer of Jesus before His battle with sin and death on the cross. As children of God, we can call on the same God who helped David and the same Father who strengthened Jesus as well.

Verse 4 is a plea for God to grant our heart's desires. As we draw near to the Lord, His will becomes our will. As we constantly abide in Him (John 15), He molds us into His own image, and we will desire His will. In verse 6 through the end of the psalm, David answers back with confidence that God will be faithful to His people. The longer we walk with the Lord, and the more we see prayer answered, the more confidence we will have in His faithfulness. Our knowledge will go past just knowing in our heads to knowing in our hearts that He is faithful. The Hebrew word here means "to know by experience." As we see the Lord answer when we call, it gives us the confidence to call again. Our God answers His people. David knew that He would answer, and Isaiah 65:24 tells us that He answers before we even call. He is faithful.

As they were going into battle, David declared that though some trusted in horses and chariots, God's people would trust in the Lord's name. So often, we are tempted to trust in the things we can see and rest our faith in the tangible. But we can trust in something so much better. The name and character of our God is so much better than anything in this world. The word here for "trust" means "to remember," and when we remember His faithfulness in the past, we can be confident that He will be faithful in the future. We know that the greatest battle has already been won at Calvary, and we know He can handle anything we face in this life. We have confidence in our almighty and faithful God, and we echo the words of Romans 8:31, "If God is for us, who is against us?"

READ VERSE 4 AND SPEND SOME TIME IN SELF-EXAMINATION. ARE YOUR HEART'S DESIRES THE SAME AS THE LORD'S? DO YOU DESIRE HIS PLANS?

REREAD VERSES 7–8. IN WHAT WAYS DOES THIS PASSAGE ILLUSTRATE THE FOOLISHNESS AND FRAILTY THAT OCCUR WHEN WE HOPE IN EARTHLY THINGS?

MEDITATE ON ROMANS 8:31. WHAT ARE SOME OF THE WAYS THAT THIS VERSE DESCRIBES THE SAME KNOWLEDGE BEING DISPLAYED THROUGH THIS PSALM?

WHAT WAS YOUR FAVORITE PASSAGE FROM THE WEEK?

Take some time to dwell on the Word by writing out the passage in the space provided.

Scripture Memory

LORD, YOU ARE MY PORTION
AND MY CUP OF BLESSING;
YOU HOLD MY FUTURE

Psalm 16:5

Week Four Reflection

SUMMARIZE THE MAIN POINTS FROM THIS WEEK'S SCRIPTURE READINGS.

WHAT DID YOU OBSERVE FROM THIS WEEK'S PASSAGES ABOUT GOD AND HIS CHARACTER?

WHAT DO THIS WEEK'S PASSAGES REVEAL ABOUT THE CONDITION OF MANKIND AND YOURSELF?

Read Psalms 16-20

HOW DO THESE PASSAGES POINT TO THE GOSPEL?

HOW SHOULD YOU RESPOND TO THESE PASSAGES? WHAT SPECIFIC ACTION STEPS CAN YOU TAKE THIS WEEK TO APPLY THEM IN YOUR LIFE?

WRITE A PRAYER IN RESPONSE TO YOUR STUDY OF GOD'S WORD. ADORE GOD FOR WHO HE IS, CONFESS SINS HE REVEALED IN YOUR OWN LIFE, ASK HIM TO EMPOWER YOU TO WALK IN OBEDIENCE, AND PRAY FOR ANYONE WHO COMES TO MIND AS YOU STUDY.

We Shall Not Be Moved

READ PSALM 21

Psalm 20 was a prayer for victory in battle, and this psalm is a song of praise after that glorious victory. In the Jewish Targum, this psalm of David was originally known as the "Psalm of King Messiah." It shows David as a type or picture of Christ, with Jesus as the ultimate and full fulfillment of the words of this psalm. This is a psalm of praise to the Lord for His faithful deliverance. Warren Wiersbe said that "answered prayers ought to be acknowledged by fervent praise." That is exactly what this psalm does. It pours out praise to the God who is faithful. We should praise Him for who He is and for what He does. He is faithful and good, and everything that He does is faithful and good.

The psalm details all the ways the Lord was faithful, and we would be wise to name His faithfulness in our lives and let it remind us to trust Him for the future. The Lord had given His people their heart's desire. The beauty of walking with the Lord is that the more we grow in Him and align our hearts with His heart, the more our hearts will desire His will. Verse 3 says that He meets with rich blessings. The word here for "meet" means "to go before." Our God goes before us, and we can have confidence in that truth no matter what we are facing in this life. With the Lord with us and before us, we will not be moved.

This life is full of battles, but our Savior has already overcome on the cross. We can go ahead confidently into battle because He goes before us, and He is with us. We can trust that the day will come when all in this world will be made right. The victory of Jesus our Messiah gives us confident faith that just as He has been faithful in the past, He will be faithful again. So we will praise His name and know that there is victory in the name of Jesus. We can remember His faithfulness and pray for Him to do it again.

THE MORE WE GROW IN HIM AND
align our hearts with His heart,
THE MORE OUR HEARTS
will desire His will.

AFTER READING THROUGH THIS PSALM, WHAT ARE SOME OF THE WAYS THAT YOU SEE IT POINT TO CHRIST?

VERSE 11 REMINDS US THAT PLANS TO THWART GOD WILL NOT SUCCEED. HOW CAN THIS GIVE YOU ENCOURAGEMENT IN YOUR EVERYDAY LIFE? DO YOU TRUST IN THE LORD'S PLANS?

HOW DOES THIS PSALM ILLUSTRATE THE CONFIDENCE WE CAN HAVE GOING INTO THE BATTLES OF LIFE? IN WHAT WAYS DOES IT GROW YOUR AFFECTION TOWARD THE LORD TO KNOW HE GOES BEFORE US?

WEEK FIVE / DAY TWO

Psalm of the Cross

Psalm of the Cross

READ PSALM 22

Psalm 22 has been called the psalm of the cross. This strikingly beautiful psalm practically speaks of Jesus in vivid detail. In a small sense, perhaps it shows the suffering of David, but it is without a doubt a psalm about the Son of David. The psalm contains many direct quotes of what Jesus said on the cross, and it is possible that He recited this while on the cross. The psalm begins with the Messiah crying out to the Lord. On the cross, the weight of our sin was placed on the spotless Son of God, which caused the Father to look away and forsake the Son for a time. This is the great exchange or the holy transaction. He took our sin so that we could take His righteousness (2 Corinthians 5:21). Yet even in His suffering, the Messiah would proclaim the holiness of Jehovah. Jesus knew that God had a holy plan and that His ways are always good. No matter how bad things seem to be, we know that God is holy. And sometimes, it is the very worst things in life that bring the very best things. The cross teaches this truth that our God can use anything for His glory and the good of His people.

The psalm continues with a detailed description of the suffering of our Savior. Verse 14 shows Jesus expressing that He is poured out, and our hearts take pause at the weight of the Living Water poured out for us. Verse 16 tells of His pierced hands and feet. David is prophetically describing the crucifixion. He had probably never seen a crucifixion as this was not a Jewish practice, and even the Romans would not begin the practice for hundreds of years. But God's plan had been set in place before the ages began. Verse 17 tells us each bone was visible and not broken as prophecy has foretold (Psalm 34:20) and as a beautiful fulfillment of Jesus as our perfect Passover Lamb (Exodus 12:46, Numbers 9:12). They stared, and they mocked our Savior, but now we gaze on the same Savior with gratitude and praise.

The tone of the psalm shifts from sorrow to joy at verse 21 because it is the sorrow of the cross that brings hope and joy to all. Our Jesus has gone to the cross to glorify the Father and because of His great love for us. He has done what we could never do on our own. The agony of the cross gives way to the triumph of the resurrection and the joy of salvation. The psalm ends with the reminder that it is finished. He has done it. Our Redeemer has paid the price for us, and now He lives.

HE TOOK OUR SIN SO THAT WE *could take His righteousness.*

THINK ABOUT THE SIMILARITIES BETWEEN THIS PSALM AND JESUS'S TIME ON THE CROSS. WHAT DOES THIS FORETELLING DISPLAY ABOUT THE NATURE AND CHARACTER OF GOD? WHY MIGHT JESUS'S RECITATION OF THIS PSALM ON THE CROSS BE IMPORTANT?

MEDITATE ON VERSE 26. IN WHAT WAYS DOES THIS VERSE GIVE YOU HOPE?

HOW DOES THE SHIFT IN THIS PSALM FROM SORROW TO JOY HELP YOU TO UNDERSTAND THE WAY IN WHICH WE SHOULD REMEMBER JESUS'S SACRIFICE FOR US?

The Lord is My Shepherd

READ PSALM 23

This psalm is one of the most well-known portions of Scripture, but we should not allow its familiarity to lessen its beauty. Its fame is for good reason, and there is perhaps no portion of Scripture that has comforted more people than this one. It begins with those famous words, "The Lord is my shepherd." Our Sovereign God has chosen to shepherd His people. The image is seen throughout the Old Testament (Genesis 48:15, 49:24, Psalm 28:9, 80:1, 95:7, 100:3, Isaiah 40:11), and Jesus would declare in John 10 that He is the Good Shepherd. He is my Shepherd because this relationship is intimate and personal. He is not just a shepherd or even the shepherd, but He is mine. We shall not want because with Jesus we have all that we need.

He makes me lie down and leads me beside still waters. The Hebrew here is literally "waters of rest." He gives rest to my soul, and then He restores my soul. He restores, or refreshes, and revives my soul. He does not have to change my circumstances to give me peace. I have peace because He is with me. I am refreshed by the water of His Word each time I come to Him. He leads me in the way I should go for my good and His glory. As the tone shifts in this psalm, we are reminded that following the Lord does not mean there will never be difficulty. But we face just the shadow of death because death was defeated on the cross, as we learned in Psalm 22. Because He is with us, we have nothing to fear. He comforts and disciplines us with His rod and staff, and we can know He will come tenderly with conviction when we stray. Then right in the midst of our troubles and our enemies, He will prepare a banquet for us and give us peace and rest. Because when we stay near our Shepherd, we can have peace and joy right in the midst of trouble. Our peace is dependent on God alone and is unchanged by the circumstances around us. He gives us fresh anointing and fills our lives until they overflow.

The psalm ends with the sweet reminder of God's constant goodness and His steadfast love. Someday we will look back on our lives and see only God's goodness and steadfast *hesed* love. Because when we finally see our life from His perspective, we will see that even our trials were met with goodness, mercy, and steadfast love. Someday, we will dwell in His house and praise Him as we see all that He has been for us. He has been our guide, our rest, our comfort, our protector, our correction, our joy, and our Lord. He is our Shepherd, and we are His sheep.

When the soul grows sorrowful, he revives it; when it is sinful he sanctifies it; when it is weak he strengthens it.

–Charles Spurgeon

HOW DOES JESUS'S PROCLAMATION THAT HE IS THE GOOD SHEPHERD TESTIFY TO HIS ONENESS WITH THE FATHER? WHY IS THIS IMPORTANT?

WHY IS IT IMPORTANT TO UNDERSTAND JESUS AS OUR SHEPHERD? WHY IS IT IMPORTANT TO UNDERSTAND OURSELVES AS HIS SHEEP?

MEDITATE ON THE COMFORT THAT IS OFFERED TO US THROUGH THIS PSALM AND REPEAT IT IN PRAYER TO GOD.

WEEK FIVE / DAY FOUR

The King of Glory

The King of Glory

READ PSALM 24

Psalm 24 is a triumphant song about our King of Glory. It was likely written to be sung at the entrance of the ark of the covenant into Jerusalem (2 Samuel 6, 1 Chronicles 15:1–16:3). The psalm begins with the declaration that the earth is the Lord's and so are all who dwell on the earth (Galatians 3:28). The psalmist then asks the question of who will ascend the hill of the Lord. The Christian life is often described as a journey or as going higher with the Lord. We long to go higher with Him and to know Him more and more. So who is it that goes higher with Him? The psalmist says it is those who have clean hands and a pure heart. Clean hands in this passage refer to our actions—this is the way that we live. A pure heart refers to our motives and our heart attitudes. It is easy to fall into the trap of doing the right things with self-serving motives, but we are urged to have not only clean hands but a pure heart as well.

The psalmist then points us to the only One who makes right living and a pure heart possible. Our gaze is shifted to the King of Glory Himself. Right living and pure motives are only possible through Jesus and His grace. He takes our sin and our selfish hearts and clothes us in His own righteousness (2 Corinthians 5:21). This is the beauty of the gospel. This psalm is thought by many to be something that would go back and forth. The question would be asked, "Who is this King of glory?" And the people would answer, "The Lord, strong and mighty." So the question is posed at the beginning of the psalm of who can be near the Lord, and then we are shown that it is the One who has been perfect in our place. The One with a pure heart and clean hands is Jesus Himself. And our hearts and hands are made clean because we are in Him. We praise our King of Glory for being righteous for us.

RIGHT LIVING AND PURE MOTIVES *are only possible through Jesus* AND HIS GRACE.

SPEND SOME TIME IN SELF-EXAMINATION REGARDING VERSE 4. WHY IS IT IMPORTANT TO HAVE CLEAN HANDS AND A PURE HEART? WHAT DOES IT LOOK LIKE TO APPEAL TO WHAT IS FALSE?

THINK ABOUT THE ANSWER TO THE QUESTION, "WHO IS THE KING OF GLORY?" WHO DO YOU SAY THE KING OF GLORY IS? HOW DOES THIS PSALM DIRECT YOUR THOUGHTS IN UNDERSTANDING THE LORD?

READ 2 CORINTHIANS 5:21. HOW DOES KNOWING THAT AT THE TIME THIS PSALM WAS WRITTEN THE ISRAELITES WERE REQUIRED TO PRACTICE OFFERINGS AND SACRIFICES TO MAINTAIN PURITY GROW YOUR UNDERSTANDING OF JESUS AS THE PERFECT SACRIFICE?

Teach Me Your Path

READ PSALM 25

This psalm is a passionate plea from the heart of David to the Lord. He comes to the Lord as the One to whom he lifts his soul—a reminder to us that our God should be the place we run to. There is no one else who will bring peace to our hearts. Even when life does not make sense, we will turn in prayer to Him and trust Him. Throughout the psalm, we see the psalmist waiting on the Lord, but he declares in verse 3 that none who wait for the Lord will be put to shame. This world may try to make us feel foolish for trusting our God, but we can be confident that our God will never fail us.

David came to the Lord in prayer in verse 1, and in verses 4–5, we see him turning to God's Word. It is on the pages of God's Word that we find His direction and will for our lives. As we wait on the Lord, we can draw near to Him in prayer and pour out our hearts. We can seek Him through His Word. David goes on to proclaim the character of God. He is again coming to the Lord to plead God's character on his behalf. We can do the same as we come to Him in prayer. He has always been faithful to us. Spurgeon said, "There shall be mercy in every unsavory morsel, and faithfulness in every bitter drop." Everything God does is evidence of His faithfulness because that is who He is. We do not always understand His ways, but we can trust that as we are following Him, even the things that seem bitter to us are mercies and faithfulness that we do not understand.

Finding God's will is about daily following the Lord, seeking Him continually, and trusting Him to direct our steps. Verse 15 reminds us to constantly set our gaze on the Lord and wait for Him. We can be confident that He will be faithful to us.

EVERYTHING GOD DOES
is evidence of His faithfulness
BECAUSE THAT IS WHO HE IS.

DO YOU FIND THAT YOU OFTEN FIRST RUN TO THE LORD WHEN YOU ARE DISTRESSED? IN WHAT WAYS DOES THIS PSALM INSTRUCT AND ENCOURAGE YOU TO SEE GOD IN PRAYER?

REFLECT ON VERSES 4 – 5. DO YOU DESIRE TO KNOW THE LORD'S WAYS? DO YOU ASPIRE TO BE LED BY HIS TRUTH? SPEND SOME TIME IN PRAYER, PRAYING THESE VERSES TO GOD.

WHAT ARE SOME PRACTICAL WAYS THAT YOU CAN FOLLOW THE LORD DAILY, SEEK HIM CONTINUALLY, AND TRUST HIM TO DIRECT YOUR STEPS?

WHAT WAS YOUR FAVORITE PASSAGE FROM THE WEEK?

Take some time to dwell on the Word by writing out the passage in the space provided.

Scripture Memory

BE EXALTED, LORD,
IN YOUR STRENGTH;
WE WILL SING AND
PRAISE YOUR MIGHT.

Psalm 21:13

Week Five Reflection

SUMMARIZE THE MAIN POINTS FROM THIS WEEK'S SCRIPTURE READINGS.

WHAT DID YOU OBSERVE FROM THIS WEEK'S PASSAGES ABOUT GOD AND HIS CHARACTER?

WHAT DO THIS WEEK'S PASSAGES REVEAL ABOUT THE CONDITION OF MANKIND AND YOURSELF?

Read Psalms 21-25

HOW DO THESE PASSAGES POINT TO THE GOSPEL?

HOW SHOULD YOU RESPOND TO THESE PASSAGES? WHAT SPECIFIC ACTION STEPS CAN YOU TAKE THIS WEEK TO APPLY THEM IN YOUR LIFE?

WRITE A PRAYER IN RESPONSE TO YOUR STUDY OF GOD'S WORD. ADORE GOD FOR WHO HE IS, CONFESS SINS HE REVEALED IN YOUR OWN LIFE, ASK HIM TO EMPOWER YOU TO WALK IN OBEDIENCE, AND PRAY FOR ANYONE WHO COMES TO MIND AS YOU STUDY.

I Love Your House

READ PSALM 26

In this psalm, David begins by begging the Lord for vindication and ends the psalm with shouts of praise. David faced many trials in his life and had many people close to him go up against him. But verse 1 tells us that he trusted the Lord without wavering. Oh, may the same be said of us! Spurgeon said, "Confidence in God is a most effectual security against sin." When we trust the Lord, it keeps us constantly near Him, away from sin, and able to trust that God is working all things for our good (Romans 8:28).

David also asked the Lord to "test" and "try" or examine him. David was seeking to live a holy life and then asking the Lord to examine his heart and mind. David said in verse 3 that God's faithful love guided him. As we remember God's great love and kindness toward us, it should lead us to holiness and repentance (Romans 2:4). His grace should not give us a license to sin, but His grace should compel us to holiness and praise (Romans 6:1-2). David points out that he did not sit with wicked or vain men. We are reminded of the importance of the people that we spend time with. It has been said that we become like the people we spend the most time with, and we should seek out relationships that point us to the Lord.

This is also when David speaks about His love for God's house. As believers, we should love the Church. Matthew Henry said, "Those who have communion with God, and delight in approaching Him, find it (the church) to be a constant pleasure, a comfortable evidence of their integrity, and a comfortable earnest of their endless felicity." Henry is essentially claiming in the last phrase that the Church should be a down payment of heaven to the believer. The Church is an imperfect glimpse of the perfect reality of heaven. Someday we will worship the Lord there with the saints of every nation and every age, and the Church today is a glimpse as we worship in diverse unity. For now, until that day, we will praise our Savior here and worship Him for who He is while we wait for His return.

HIS GRACE SHOULD

compel us to

HOLINESS AND PRAISE.

WHAT MIGHT IT LOOK LIKE TO WALK WITH INTEGRITY AND TRUST THE LORD WITHOUT WAVERING? WHY IS IT IMPORTANT TO DO SO?

REREAD VERSES 4 – 5. WHY SHOULD WE CONTINUALLY EXAMINE WHO WE FELLOWSHIP WITH? WHY IS IT CRUCIAL TO SURROUND OURSELVES WITH OTHER BELIEVERS?

WHAT DOES IT MEAN TO LOVE THE HOUSE WHERE THE LORD DWELLS, AS STATED IN VERSE 8? WHY SHOULD WE DWELL SO CLOSELY WITH THE LORD?

WEEK SIX / DAY TWO

I Will Seek You

I Will Seek You

READ PSALM 27

No matter what is happening in our lives, whatever situation we may find ourselves in, we can trust in the Lord. In this psalm, David speaks of his confidence in the Lord. We know that David's life was not always easy, and yet still, he trusted the Lord. David knew in his soul that with God on his side, he had nothing to fear (Romans 8:31). We need not ever fear or worry about what might happen or the foes that are against us. So often, we are prone to worry about what could happen, but David tells us that we have nothing to fear.

David then shifts his focus in verses 4–6 with what Wiersbe says is equal to the New Testament concept of abiding in Christ (John 15). Our hearts should desire and seek after the Lord. We should long to dwell, or abide, with Him and gaze on Him, meditating on who He is. Verse 5 reminds us that we should desire Him and seek after Him because He will be faithful to us. He will be our shelter even when our situation seems hopeless. As the Lord asks all of His people to seek Him, our individual hearts echo back to Him that we will do His will. If He has told us to seek, we will seek. If he has told us to go, we will go. And if He has told us to wait, we will wait. The word here for "seek" in Hebrew is *baqash* and can mean "to seek, to find." It is a sweet reminder that when we seek Him, we will find Him (Jeremiah 29:13). May the cry of our hearts be, "I will seek You." And we can have full confidence that we will find Him.

David ends the psalm with the passionate declaration that he knows that God will be faithful to him. We can live with that same confidence that our God will be faithful to us. So whatever situation we find ourselves in, we can confidently wait on the Lord, knowing that He will be faithful. We expect and await and look eagerly for Him because we know that He will never fail us.

OUR HEARTS SHOULD DESIRE
and seek after the Lord.

WHAT DOES VERSE 4 REVEAL ABOUT WHAT DAVID FOUND THE MOST VALUABLE? DO YOU ALSO FIND THAT YOU DESIRE AND VALUE DWELLING WITH THE LORD AND APPRECIATING HIS BEAUTY?

MEDITATE ON VERSE 14. WHY IS IT IMPORTANT TO WAIT ON THE LORD AND REMAIN STRONG AND COURAGEOUS IN DOING SO?

DO YOU FIND IT CHALLENGING TO WAIT ON THE LORD AND TRUST HIM? AS YOU REFLECT ON THIS PSALM, SPEND SOME TIME IN PRAYER, ASKING THAT GOD WOULD STRENGTHEN YOUR FAITH AND TRUST IN HIS TIMING.

In Him My Heart Trusts

READ PSALM 28

Delay does not mean defeat. Just because the Lord has us in a season of waiting does not mean that He is not working. He is working in the waiting. In this psalm, David cries to the Lord and pleads with the Lord to hear and be faithful to him. It is to the Lord alone that we cry out because we know that He will listen. And after He has listened, in His timing, we can be sure that He will act.

We reflect with David about where we would be without the Lord, and we take comfort that He is with us. We plead with Him to hear, and then we lift up our empty hands to Him. Spurgeon says, "We lift up empty hands for we are beggars; we lift them up because we seek heavenly supplies; we lift them toward the mercy seat of Jesus, for there our expectation dwells." Our God is our only hope, so we come to Him with expectation. We look at the situation we are in, no matter how bad it may be, and then we look expectantly for just a glimpse of how He is already working. We know He is working, so we search for that glimmer of His grace right in our mess. Like watching a pot of water about to boil, it sometimes seems we wait so long, but sure enough, every pot of water on a hot stove will boil, and every situation in our lives will be evidence of grace. So we wait with anticipation for those first bubbles to rise to the surface as a sweet reminder that He is working.

As the psalm moves on, we see God's justice over wickedness. Right now, we plead for God's mercy on men, but someday we will also be comforted by His justice over sin. Then David's prayer turns to praise. It is the kind of praise made rich by seeing and experiencing God's steadfast love and faithfulness through the years. Our God is our strength and our shield, our Protector. In verse 7, we see that as we place our trust in Him, we are helped.

First, we trust, and then we triumph. The psalm ends with David pleading God's character—and we can do the same. We acknowledge and praise God for who He is and then ask Him to do it for us. David turned his problems into prayer and his prayers into praise. Oh, that we would do the same.

JUST BECAUSE THE LORD HAS US
in a season of waiting does not mean
THAT HE IS NOT WORKING.

REFLECT ON THE VERY FIRST LINE OF THIS PSALM. DO YOU MAKE IT A HABIT TO CALL ON THE LORD IN PRAYER? WHY IS THIS AN IMPORTANT DISCIPLINE IN THE CHRISTIAN LIFE?

WHAT DOES IT LOOK LIKE FOR US TO KNOW THAT THE LORD IS OUR STRENGTH AND SHIELD? HOW DOES THIS CHANGE THE WAY WE EXPERIENCE DIFFICULTY AND TRIALS?

IN THE LAST LINE, WE SEE THE LORD REFERRED TO AS A SHEPHERD. HOW DOES THIS PSALM EXPAND YOUR UNDERSTANDING OF THE ANALOGY THAT GOD IS OUR SHEPHERD AND WE ARE HIS SHEEP?

WEEK SIX / DAY FOUR

Sing in the Storm

Sing in the Storm

READ PSALM 29

The child of God can sing in the storm. No matter what may come, we can praise Him. The psalm opens with the call to ascribe to the Lord glory. With the angels above, we are called to pour out our worship to our God. We are called to give Him the glory due to His name. Our mortal tongues could never fully give Him the worship that He deserves, so we pour out our worship as best as we can and as often as we can. As we grow in holiness, we are constantly seeking to take our eyes off ourselves and fix our eyes on Him. All of nature proclaims His praise, and even the storms of this life proclaim His majesty.

In nature and in Scripture, God's voice is powerful. His Word has the power to change, comfort, encourage, convict, and bring to life. Nature points to our God and should produce worship from His people. Even after the thunder and the storm, if the floodwaters come, He is not alarmed because He is in control of it all. The child of God can sing in the storm because we know the master of the storm. The master of the storm brings peace to the storm and peace to our hearts. The thunders of life's storms will only turn our hearts to the thunder of His voice. It is Him alone who calms the hearts of His people, who gives strength to their souls, and who fills them with His peace. He gives us shalom peace right in the midst of the storm. He gives us confidence in who He is. We give Him glory, and He gives us peace. He gives us strength and peace because He gives us Himself—and that is all we will ever need.

ALL OF NATURE PROCLAIMS HIS PRAISE,
and even the storms of this life
PROCLAIM HIS MAJESTY.

LOOK UP THE DEFINITION FOR THE WORD "ASCRIBE."
HOW DOES THIS DEFINITION HELP YOU UNDERSTAND THIS PSALM?

IN WHAT WAYS HAS THIS CHAPTER GROWN YOUR UNDERSTANDING OF THE POWER OF GOD? HOW DOES THIS DESCRIPTION OF GOD'S VOICE GROW YOUR UNDERSTANDING OF THE POWER WITHIN THE WORD OF GOD, OUR BIBLES?

MEDITATE ON VERSE 10. WHY IS IT IMPORTANT FOR US TO REMEMBER THE LORD ON HIS THRONE?

Joy Comes in the Morning

READ PSALM 30

Glory to thee for all the grace I have not tasted yet.

–Charles Spurgeon

This beautiful psalm of David is titled as a song at the dedication of the temple. It would be easy to skip over this title, but it holds great significance because David had passed away at the time the temple was dedicated, but God had promised him that Solomon, his son, would complete it. This is a song of faith to a faithful God. David knew that God would be faithful, so he wrote this psalm as if it had already happened. What an example to us to start praising God even before we see the fulfillment of His promises because we know that He will be faithful.

In this psalm, David reminds us that he had faced many difficulties. Foes had come against him, and his own sin and despair had caused him to walk through some dark days. But the Lord was there every step of the way. David lifted God up because God had lifted David up. David lifted the Lord up in praise because God had lifted David up out of despair. The psalm proclaims the theme that our weeping and sorrow and trouble will last for but a moment. The night will not last forever, and morning will break through just like the power of God's grace and mercy in our lives. Jesus Himself would speak much the same words in John 16:20 when He promised the disciples that He would turn, or transform, their sorrow into joy. That is the power of the resurrection.

In pride, David had once thought that he would never be moved, as we so often do, but God in His mercy would do what was best for David and for us as well. God allows us to face both weeping and joy because He knows what is best for us. Someday, we will be able to look back on our lives and say, "only goodness and faithful love," just as David did in Psalm 23, because our God uses everything for our good (Romans 8:28). Our mourning will be turned to dancing, our sackcloth will be exchanged for gladness, and our hearts will respond in praise to Him. The little word "that" at the beginning of verse 12 reminds us of the purpose even in our suffering. We are going to face suffering, and He is going to be faithful. There will be dark nights, but the sun will surely rise. And it will all happen "so that" everything we are will praise Him. We will see Him in our suffering and be utterly convinced that His faithfulness has led us all the way. And like David, we can sing and pray these words in faith. He is faithful. We know that He will be faithful to us.

START PRAISING GOD EVEN BEFORE
we see the fulfillment of His promises.

HOW DOES THE CONTEXT OF THIS PSALM ENCOURAGE YOU OF GOD'S FAITHFULNESS? ARE YOU WILLING TO PRAISE HIM AND THANK HIM FOR WHAT HE HAS DONE, EVEN IF YOU HAVE NOT SEEN THE FULL PICTURE?

MEDITATE ON VERSE 11. IN WHAT WAYS HAS THE LORD TURNED YOUR OWN LAMENT INTO DANCING?

NOW THAT WE HAVE FINISHED STUDYING THE FIRST THIRTY PSALMS, REFLECT ON ALL THAT YOU HAVE LEARNED. WHAT ARE SOME OF THE WAYS GOD HAS GROWN YOUR KNOWLEDGE OF HIM AND HIS WORD THROUGH THE PSALMS?

WHAT WAS YOUR FAVORITE PASSAGE FROM THE WEEK?

Take some time to dwell on the Word by writing out the passage in the space provided.

Scripture Memory

THE LORD IS MY LIGHT
AND MY SALVATION —
WHOM SHOULD I FEAR?
THE LORD IS THE STRONGHOLD
OF MY LIFE —
WHOM SHOULD I DREAD?

Psalm 27:1

Week Six Reflection

SUMMARIZE THE MAIN POINTS FROM THIS WEEK'S SCRIPTURE READINGS.

WHAT DID YOU OBSERVE FROM THIS WEEK'S PASSAGES ABOUT GOD AND HIS CHARACTER?

WHAT DO THIS WEEK'S PASSAGES REVEAL ABOUT THE CONDITION OF MANKIND AND YOURSELF?

Read Psalms 26-30

HOW DO THESE PASSAGES POINT TO THE GOSPEL?

HOW SHOULD YOU RESPOND TO THESE PASSAGES? WHAT SPECIFIC ACTION STEPS CAN YOU TAKE THIS WEEK TO APPLY THEM IN YOUR LIFE?

WRITE A PRAYER IN RESPONSE TO YOUR STUDY OF GOD'S WORD. ADORE GOD FOR WHO HE IS, CONFESS SINS HE REVEALED IN YOUR OWN LIFE, ASK HIM TO EMPOWER YOU TO WALK IN OBEDIENCE, AND PRAY FOR ANYONE WHO COMES TO MIND AS YOU STUDY.

What is *the* Gospel?

Thank you for reading and enjoying this study with us! We are abundantly grateful for the Word of God, the instruction we glean from it, and the ever-growing understanding it provides for us of God's character. We are also thankful that Scripture continually points to one thing in innumerable ways: the gospel.

We remember our brokenness when we read about the fall of Adam and Eve in the garden of Eden (Genesis 3), where sin entered into a perfect world and maimed it. We remember the necessity that something innocent must die to pay for our sin when we read about the atoning sacrifices in the Old Testament. We read that we have all sinned and fallen short of the glory of God (Romans 3:23) and that the penalty for our brokenness, the wages of our sin, is death (Romans 6:23). We all need grace and mercy, but most importantly, we all need a Savior.

We consider the goodness of God when we realize that He did not plan to leave us in this dire state. We see His promise to buy us back from the clutches of sin and death in Genesis 3:15. And we see that promise accomplished with Jesus Christ on the cross. Jesus Christ knew no sin yet became sin so that we might become righteous through His sacrifice (2 Corinthians 5:21). Jesus was tempted in every way that we are and lived sinlessly. He was reviled yet still yielded Himself for our sake, that we may have life abundant in Him. Jesus lived the perfect life that we could not live and died the death that we deserved.

The gospel is profound yet simple. There are many mysteries in it that we will never understand this side of heaven, but there is still overwhelming weight to its implications in this life. The gospel tells of our sinfulness and God's goodness and a gracious gift that compels a response. We are saved by grace through faith, which means that we rest with faith in the grace that Jesus Christ displayed on the cross (Ephesians 2:8–9). We cannot save ourselves from our brokenness or do any amount of good works to merit God's favor. Still, we can have faith that what Jesus accomplished in His death, burial, and resurrection was more than enough for our salvation and our eternal delight. When we accept God, we are commanded to die to ourselves and our sinful desires and live a life worthy of the calling we have received (Ephesians 4:1). The gospel compels us to be sanctified, and in so doing, we are conformed to the likeness of Christ Himself. This is hope. This is redemption. This is the gospel.

GENESIS 3:15

I will put hostility between you and the woman, and between your offspring and her offspring. He will strike your head, and you will strike his heel.

ROMANS 3:23

For all have sinned and fall short of the glory of God.

ROMANS 6:23

For the wages of sin is death, but the gift of God is eternal life in Christ Jesus our Lord.

2 CORINTHIANS 5:21

He made the one who did not know sin to be sin for us, so that in him we might become the righteousness of God.

EPHESIANS 2:8–9

For you are saved by grace through faith, and this is not from yourselves; it is God's gift—not from works, so that no one can boast.

EPHESIANS 4:1–3

Therefore I, the prisoner in the Lord, urge you to walk worthy of the calling you have received, with all humility and gentleness, with patience, bearing with one another in love, making every effort to keep the unity of the Spirit through the bond of peace.

BIBLIOGRAPHY

Kidner, Derek. *Psalms 1–72.* Kidner Classic Commentaries. Westmont, IL: IVP Academic, 2014.

Longman III, Tremper. *Psalms: An Introduction and Commentary.* Tyndale Old Testament Commentaries 15–16. Westmont, IL: IVP Academic, 2014.

Longman III, Tremper, and David E. Garland, ed. Psalms. Vol. 5 of *The Expositor's Bible Commentary.* Grand Rapids, MI: Zondervan Academic, 2015.

Spurgeon, Charles Haddon. *The Treasury of David.* 3 vols. Peabody, MA: Hendrickson Publishers, 1988.

Wilcock, Michael. *The Message of Psalms 1–71: Psalms for the People of God.* The Bible Speaks Today Series. Westmont, IL: IVP Academic, 2001.

Thank you for studying God's Word with us!

CONNECT WITH US

@thedailygraceco
@dailygracepodcast

CONTACT US

info@thedailygraceco.com

SHARE

#thedailygraceco

VISIT US ONLINE

www.thedailygraceco.com

MORE DAILY GRACE

The Daily Grace App
Daily Grace Podcast